Felicity's COOKING STUDIO

TABLE *of* CONTENTS

FELICITY'S KITCHEN PAGE 5

TIPS FOR TODAY'S COOKS
HANDY HINTS

BREAKFAST PAGE 11

APPLE BUTTER
JOHNNYCAKES
BREAKFAST PUFFS
FRIED HAM WITH GRAVY
DRESSED EGGS

DINNER PAGE 23

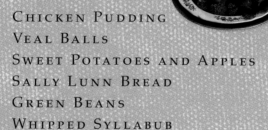

CHICKEN PUDDING
VEAL BALLS
SWEET POTATOES AND APPLES
SALLY LUNN BREAD
GREEN BEANS
WHIPPED SYLLABUB

FAVORITE FOODS PAGE 35

BEEFSTEAK PIE
BAKED PUMPKIN PUDDING
RASPBERRY FLUMMERY
ALMOND TARTS
SPICED NUTS
LIBERTY TEA

PARTY IDEAS PAGE 45

COLONIAL TEA
TWELFTH NIGHT BALL
PLANTATION PICNIC

I n colonial Virginia, families prided themselves on their warm hospitality. Virginians were always prepared for unexpected guests, and they welcomed friends, family members, and travelers into their homes with lots of good food.

All that good food took a long time to make. There were no stoves, refrigerators, or running water in colonial times. Cooking was a hot, tiring task that was usually done by servants and slaves. Girls like Felicity didn't have to cook meals for their families. They learned to cook so that they could direct the work of servants and slaves and manage a household of their own one day.

Cooks in the late 1700s usually worked over an open fire in the kitchen fireplace. Meat and vegetables were often boiled in large pots and kettles. Cooks controlled the temperature by moving pots closer to or farther from the flames. Meat might also be roasted on a *spit*, a rod for holding meat over a fire. The meat had to be turned constantly so it would cook evenly. Bread was often baked in a small, brick-lined oven in the wall next to the fireplace. To check the oven temperature, a cook would hold her arm in the oven. If she could count to 30, but no higher, before having to remove her arm, the oven was hot enough.

A colonial bread toaster

As you try the recipes in *Felicity's Cooking Studio*, you'll discover what kitchens, cooking, and growing up were like in Felicity's time. You may even discover that some of Felicity's favorite treats are your favorites, too.

COLONIAL COOKING

Kitchen Hazards

Cooking pots were often hung from a rod attached at the back of the fireplace. Wealthy families could afford metal rods, but less fortunate families used green poles, or newly cut wood poles. Green poles burned slowly because the sap in the wood made them wet. Even so, green poles did burn through eventually and had to be replaced.

Cooking in Felicity's time was much different from cooking today. Kitchens did not have built-in sinks, refrigerators, stoves, or microwaves. The kitchen wasn't even part of the main house. It was a *dependency*, or an outbuilding separate from the main house. This arrangement kept cooking heat and odors from reaching the house. It also separated the family from their servants and slaves.

Kitchens were filled with cupboards, storage chests, and barrels. Large flat boards laid over the chests and barrels made good work surfaces. One wall of the kitchen had a large fireplace that was used mainly for cooking food, but it also heated the room. The fireplace was so big that Felicity could stand up in it! A colonial cook kept the kitchen fire burning all day long, all year round. The constant flames made wood floors a fire hazard, so kitchen floors were made of brick or packed earth.

A *kitchen garden* supplied the Merrimans with all their produce. Vegetables, melons, pumpkins, and squash grew in tidy rows along with fresh herbs. Cooks gathered the herbs and dried them in bunches to use throughout the year.

Many of the dishes and pieces of furniture that Felicity's family used were brought with them from England, or were made there and shipped to the colonists in Virginia. Eventually, colonists began making these things themselves, and soon the quality of goods made in the colonies matched the quality of imported items. A merchant family like the Merrimans might have had dishes from England or China as well as plates, bowls, and platters made in the colonies.

Tables often had two layers of table coverings. Servants first laid a heavy cloth on the table. Then they laid a fine white linen tablecloth over that. Straw or cane mats were set under serving dishes to protect the white tablecloth from food drippings.

Plates, glasses, and utensils were arranged the same way you set a table today. Soup bowls were placed in front of the hostess so that she could serve each person. Linen napkins were put at each place, usually right on the plate. Sometimes a dinner roll was tucked inside the napkin. Some wealthy women and girls folded napkins into fancy shapes to add the perfect finishing touch to the table.

Hand-Painted Dishes

Some very wealthy families ordered special sets of painted dishes from China. A landowner might send a sketch of his plantation so that it could be painted onto his china. Sometimes the dishes came back with the plantation sitting in a field of bamboo or next to a temple that never would have existed in the colonies!

Here is a list of tips that every good cook should know. But this is the most important tip: **work with an adult.** This is the safe way for you to work in the kitchen.

When you see this symbol, it means you will need an adult's help with that step.

Colonial Measurements

There were no standard measuring cups and spoons in Felicity's time. Instead, recipes called for ingredients by weight. A good set of scales and weights was one of the most important pieces of kitchen equipment a colonial cook could have.

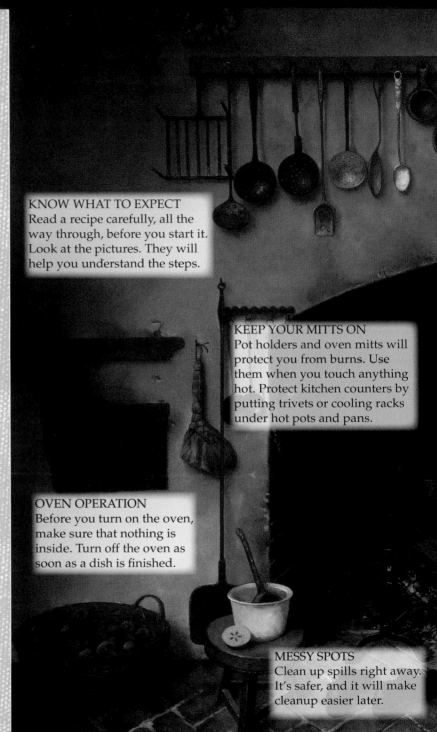

KNOW WHAT TO EXPECT
Read a recipe carefully, all the way through, before you start it. Look at the pictures. They will help you understand the steps.

KEEP YOUR MITTS ON
Pot holders and oven mitts will protect you from burns. Use them when you touch anything hot. Protect kitchen counters by putting trivets or cooling racks under hot pots and pans.

OVEN OPERATION
Before you turn on the oven, make sure that nothing is inside. Turn off the oven as soon as a dish is finished.

MESSY SPOTS
Clean up spills right away. It's safer, and it will make cleanup easier later.

Felicity's
COOKING STUDIO

SELECT A SIZE

Make sure your mixing bowls, pots, and pans are the right size. If they are too small, you'll probably spill. If pots and pans are too large, foods will burn more easily.

CLEAN GREENS

Wash all fruits and vegetables thoroughly before you use them.

Handy Hints

MEASURING FLOUR

A good cook measures exactly. Here is a hint for measuring flour. Spoon the flour into a measuring cup, heaping it up over the top. Then use the spoon handle to level off the flour. Do not shake or tap the cup.

TABLE OF MEASUREMENTS

3 teaspoons	=	1 tablespoon
2 cups	=	1 pint
2 pints	=	1 quart
4 cups	=	1 quart

TIMING

When a recipe gives two cooking times—for example, when it says "bake 25 to 30 minutes"—first set the timer for the shorter time. If the food is not done when the timer rings, give it more time.

CUTTING AND CHOPPING

*Ask an adult to show you how to peel, cut, and grate with sharp kitchen tools. Use a cutting board so that you don't damage kitchen counters. **Always use a separate board for raw meat or poultry.***

STIRRING AND MIXING

When you stir or mix, hold the bowl or pan steady on a flat surface, not in your arms.

GET READY
Gather all the ingredients and equipment you will need before you start to cook. Put everything where you can reach it easily.

BEFORE YOU START
Wash your hands with soap and warm water before and after you handle food. Wear an apron, tie back your hair, remove jewelry, and roll up your sleeves.

DRY YOUR HANDS
Never touch an electrical plug or a socket with wet hands.

BEFORE YOU FINISH
Cleanup is part of cooking, too. Leave the kitchen at least as clean as you found it. Wash all the dishes, pots, and pans. Sweep the floor. Throw away the garbage.

KNIFE KNOW-HOW
Pay attention while using knives so that you don't cut your fingers! Have an adult make sure that the knife is sharp. A sharp knife is easier to use —and safer—than a dull one.

TEMPERATURE MATTERS
Keep hot foods hot and cold foods cold. If you plan to make things ahead and serve them later, store them properly. Food that could spoil belong in the refrigerator. Wrap foods well.

STOVE SMARTS
Don't use the stove burners or the oven without permission. Always ask an adult to handle hot, heavy pans or boiling liquids.

Breakfast

Apple Butter

•

Johnnycakes

•

Breakfast Puffs

•

Fried Ham with Gravy

•

Dressed Eggs

Colonial breakfasts were served between eight and nine o'clock in the morning. In wealthy families, girls and women like Felicity and her mother did not usually prepare breakfast. Instead, slaves like Rose got up as early as 5:30 A.M. to rekindle the fire, haul water, and begin cooking breakfast for the family. Rose began by baking the breakfast bread.

She heated the *Dutch oven*, or bake kettle, in the fireplace. It had short legs to keep the bread above the hot coals. While the bread was baking, Rose heated the griddle to make johnnycakes and breakfast puffs. Then she fixed meat left over from dinner the day before. Rose made dressed eggs by broiling them. First, she heated a *salamander*, or long-handled shovel, in the fire until it was red-hot. Then she cracked the eggs into a frying pan and cooked them over the fire. When the eggs were set but not hard, she held the salamander over the eggs to cook the tops.

When everything was ready, Rose brought the food from the kitchen to a *sideboard* in the dining room. A sideboard is a piece of furniture that is used for serving food. It also has drawers or shelves which hold linens and china. Felicity sometimes helped Rose at the sideboard by taking the food from the kitchen bowls and platters and putting it onto fine china for the table.

APPLE BUTTER

Makes 2 pints

Ingredients

- 3 cups apple cider
- 2 pounds apples (about 6 large apples)
- ¼ cup honey
- ½ teaspoon cinnamon
- ¼ teaspoon ground cloves
- ¼ teaspoon allspice

Equipment

- Measuring cups and spoons
- Large cooking pot with lid
- Paring knife
- Cutting board
- Wooden spoon
- Potato masher
- 4 empty jam jars with lids, 8 ounces each
- Paper towels

Spread sweet apple butter on your favorite breakfast bread.

Directions

1. Measure the cider into the cooking pot. Cook the cider over medium heat until it *boils*, or bubbles quickly. Let the cider boil for 15 minutes.

2. While the cider boils, have an adult help you cut each apple into 4 sections.

3. Have an adult help you remove the core from each section and cut off the skin. Then cut the apple sections into small pieces.

4. Carefully add the apples to the boiling cider.

5. Cover the cooking pot. Cook the apples over very low heat until they are tender, about 1 hour. Stir the apples often while they cook.

6. Turn off the heat and remove the lid from the pot. Have an adult help you use the potato masher to mash the apples.

7. Stir in the honey, cinnamon, cloves, and allspice.

8. Turn the heat to low. Cook the apple mixture uncovered for about 30 minutes, or until it thickens. Stir often.

9. Turn off the heat and let the apple butter cool for 15 minutes in the pot.

10. While the apple butter cools, wash the jars in hot, soapy water. Then rinse them in hot water. Drain them on paper towels.

11. With an adult's help, spoon the apple butter into the jars. Serve apple butter on johnnycakes (page 14) or breakfast puffs (page 16). Store the rest of the apple butter in the refrigerator.

Keeping Foods Cold

Since colonists didn't have refrigerators, they kept foods like milk and butter cool in a **dependency**, *or outbuilding, called a* **dairy**. *A dairy was sometimes built a foot or two below ground level, usually over a cool spring. Thick walls under a big, overhanging roof kept the cool air inside. Vents let hot air escape.*

JOHNNYCAKES

Makes 12 cakes

Ingredients

- 1 cup water
- 2 tablespoons butter
- 1 cup yellow cornmeal
- ½ teaspoon salt
- ½ teaspoon sugar
- ½ cup milk
- Butter to grease skillet
- Apple butter or your favorite syrup

Equipment

- Measuring cups and spoons
- Small saucepan
- Medium mixing bowl
- Pot holder
- Wooden spoon
- Paper towels
- 12-inch skillet
- Spatula
- Ovenproof plate

Johnnycakes were also called "journey cakes" because they kept well on long trips.

Directions ✋ *Have an adult help you with **all** the steps in this recipe.*

1. Heat the water and butter in the saucepan over medium-high heat until they *boil*, or bubble rapidly.

2. While the water and butter are boiling, put the cornmeal, salt, and sugar into the mixing bowl.

3. Pour the boiling water and butter into the mixing bowl. Add the milk and stir the batter until it is well mixed.

4. Use paper towels to grease the skillet with butter. Then heat the skillet over medium-low heat.

5. Drop 6 spoonfuls of batter into the skillet. Let the cakes cook about 5 minutes, until they are golden brown.

6. Use the spatula to turn over the cakes. Let the other side of each cake cook for another 5 minutes.

7. Use the spatula to move the cakes from the skillet to an ovenproof plate. Keep them warm in a 200° oven.

8. Drop a spoonful of butter into the hot skillet and let it melt. Tilt the pan to coat the bottom of the skillet evenly with the melted butter.

9. Cook the rest of the johnnycakes following steps 5 through 7.

10. When all the cakes are cooked, serve them with apple butter (page 12) or syrup.

Corn in the Colonies

American Indians taught colonists how to grow corn. Some fresh corn was eaten right off the cob or mixed into stews. But corn was usually dried and ground into cornmeal for bread. American Indians also made popcorn, which they sometimes served with maple syrup.

Indian women scaring crows out of their cornfields

BREAKFAST PUFFS

Makes 12 puffs

Ingredients

- Shortening, butter, or cooking spray to grease muffin pan
- 1 tablespoon butter
- 2 eggs
- 1 cup milk
- 1 cup flour
- ¼ teaspoon salt
- Apple butter, jam, or honey (optional)

Equipment

- Paper towels
- Muffin pan
- Measuring cups and spoons
- Small saucepan
- Small mixing bowl
- Fork
- Mixing spoon
- Medium mixing bowl
- Pot holders
- Butter knife
- Serving plate

Serve these puffs while they're still warm from the oven.

Directions

1. Preheat the oven to 425°.

2. Use paper towels to grease the muffin cups with shortening or butter, or coat the cups with cooking spray. Put the muffin pan in the oven to heat.

3. Have an adult help you melt 1 tablespoon of butter in the small saucepan over low heat.

4. While the butter melts, crack the eggs into the small mixing bowl. Use the fork to beat the eggs until they are light yellow.

5. Add the milk and melted butter to the eggs. Beat the liquid mixture with the fork until it is well mixed. Set aside.

6. Stir the flour and salt together in the medium mixing bowl.

7. Slowly stir the liquid mixture into the flour mixture. Stir only until the batter is blended. Do not overmix.

8. With an adult's help, remove the hot muffin pan from the oven. Spoon batter into the muffin pan until each cup is ⅔ full. Have an adult put the muffin pan back into the oven.

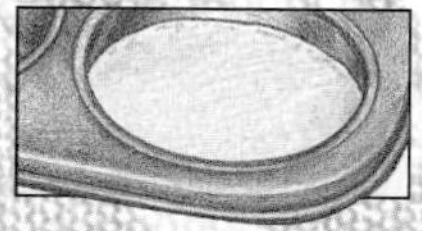

9. Bake the breakfast puffs at 425° for 20 minutes. Then turn the heat down to 325° and bake the puffs for 15 minutes.

10. Have an adult remove the breakfast puffs from the oven. Use a butter knife to loosen the sides of the breakfast puffs and remove them from the muffin cups.

11. Arrange the breakfast puffs on a serving plate. Serve the puffs with apple butter (page 12), jam, or honey.

Plate Warmers

Plate warmers like this one warmed plates before food was put on them. The open back that you see here was put in front of a fireplace. Plates were removed through a door visible on the other side of the warmer.

FRIED HAM WITH GRAVY

Serves 6

Ingredients

- 1 pound smoked ham slice
- ½ cup cold water
- 2 tablespoons fresh-brewed coffee

Equipment

- Sharp knife
- Cutting board
- Large skillet
- Fork
- Serving plate
- Aluminum foil
- Metal container for grease
- Measuring cup and spoon
- Wooden spoon

In 1774, smoked hams were a specialty in Virginia, just as they are today.

Directions  *Have an adult help you with **all** the steps in this recipe.*

1. Cut the ham slice into serving-size pieces.

2. Warm the skillet over medium-low heat.

3. Add the ham pieces and fry them over low heat.

4. Use the fork to turn over the ham pieces several times to brown both sides evenly.

5. Use the fork to move the fried ham pieces onto the serving plate.

6. Cover the plate with aluminum foil to keep the ham warm.

7. If there is grease in the frying pan, have an adult pour it off into a metal container. Leave the drippings that are stuck to the bottom of the pan.

8. To make the gravy, pour the cold water and coffee over the drippings in the skillet.

9. Turn the heat to medium and stir the gravy mixture constantly.

10. When the gravy begins to *boil*, or bubble quickly, turn off the heat.

11. Remove the aluminum foil from the serving plate.

12. Pour the gravy over the ham pieces before serving. ❧

Smokehouses

After butchering, meat was salted and then smoked in a smokehouse to help preserve it. Colonists used slow-burning fuel like corncobs for the fire. The meat took on the flavor of the fuel used. Families stored their meat in smokehouses until they needed it.

Colonial Pigs

In Felicity's time, pigs had long snouts, large tusks, and a ridge of bristles down their backs. Their owners often let them run wild! One man's pigs got into a crop of peanuts. The meat from these pigs was delicious, and soon peanut-fed ham was in high demand.

Hog

DRESSED EGGS

Serves 6

Ingredients

- ¼ cup butter
- 6 eggs
- Salt
- 1 tablespoon water
- Nutmeg

Equipment

- Measuring cup and spoon
- Skillet or dish with lid (flameproof and ovenproof)
- Small cup
- Pot holders
- Trivet
- Spatula

These eggs are "dressed" with a dash of nutmeg.

Directions

*Have an adult help you with **all** the steps in this recipe.*

1. Preheat the oven to broil.

2. Melt the butter in the skillet or dish over low heat. Don't let the butter burn.

3. Measure 1 tablespoon of melted butter into the small cup. Set the cup aside.

4. Tilt the skillet or dish to spread the remaining melted butter evenly over the bottom of the pan.

5. Carefully crack the eggs into the skillet or dish. Try not to break the yolks.

6. Shake a little salt over the eggs. Then add the water.

7. Cover the skillet or dish and cook the eggs over low heat until the whites are set but not hard, about 5 minutes.

8. Remove the lid and pour the tablespoon of melted butter evenly over the eggs.

9. Put the skillet or dish under the broiler.

10. Cook the eggs for about 1 minute. Check them after 30 seconds. The yolks should be set on top.

11. Remove the skillet or dish from the oven. Sprinkle nutmeg on the eggs.

12. Place the skillet or dish on a trivet at the table and use a spatula to serve the eggs. 🌿

Eggs and Chickens

One colonial cake recipe called for 30 eggs! That seems like a lot of eggs, but 30 eggs in Felicity's time isn't the same as 30 eggs today. Chickens were much smaller then, and their eggs were smaller, too.

DINNER

Chicken Pudding

•

Veal Balls

•

Sweet Potatoes and Apples

•

Sally Lunn Bread

•

Green Beans

•

Whipped Syllabub

In colonial times, girls like Felicity learned the art of *housewifery*, or how to manage a household, from their mothers. As part of their training, girls learned how to plan and serve elegant dinners. In Felicity's time, people ate dinner, the biggest meal of the day, between two and three o'clock in the afternoon. Shortly before bedtime, they ate supper—a smaller, simpler meal.

Hospitality was an important part of being a fine gentlewoman in Virginia. If the Merrimans had visitors, Mrs. Merriman invited them to stay for dinner. She always made sure there was plenty of food in case unexpected guests stopped by.

An everyday dinner usually had two courses, with five dishes in each course. For large dinner parties, there might be as many as 21 dishes in each course! The first course might include meats, vegetables, soup, and bread. The second course included desserts like custard or whipped syllabub.

Mrs. Merriman also taught Felicity how to arrange the table. In the English tradition, it was proper to set a balanced table. If there was a meat dish at one end of the table, there was a meat dish at the other end of the table to balance it. Pairs of matching bowls or platters were placed so that the table matched from side to side and corner to corner, too. After the meal, a hostess might serve more sweets. Dishes or pyramids of foods like dried fruits or candied flower petals might be arranged on a raised platform on the table called a *middleboard*.

A middleboard

CHICKEN PUDDING

Serves 6

Ingredients

- 2 tablespoons butter
- 2 pounds boneless, skinless chicken breasts
- 2 cups water
- 1 teaspoon salt
- Shortening, butter, or cooking spray to grease casserole dish
- 1½ cups flour
- 1 teaspoon salt
- 1½ teaspoons baking soda
- 3 tablespoons butter
- 3 eggs
- 1½ cups milk

Equipment

- Measuring cups and spoons
- Large skillet with lid
- Tongs
- Paper towels
- 2-quart casserole dish
- Small mixing bowl
- Wooden spoon
- Small saucepan
- Large mixing bowl
- Pot holders
- Trivet
- Serving spoon

In 1774, puddings were served both as main dishes and as desserts.

Directions

✋ **1.** Have an adult help you melt 2 tablespoons of butter in the skillet over medium heat.

✋ **2.** Add the chicken breasts to the skillet. With an adult's help, cook the chicken, turning the pieces with tongs until the chicken is lightly browned on both sides.

3. Measure the water and 1 teaspoon of salt into the skillet. When the water *boils*, or bubbles quickly, turn down the heat until the water *simmers*, or bubbles gently.

4. Cover the skillet and cook the chicken for 30 minutes.

5. Use paper towels to grease the casserole dish with shortening or butter, or coat the dish with cooking spray.

6. With an adult's help, use tongs to put the cooked chicken breasts into the casserole. Preheat the oven to 375°.

7. To make the batter for the chicken pudding, put the flour, salt, and baking soda into the small mixing bowl and stir them until they are well blended.

8. Have an adult help you melt 3 tablespoons of butter in the small saucepan over low heat.

9. Crack the eggs into the large mixing bowl and beat them together with the milk. Have an adult help you stir the melted butter into the eggs and milk.

10. Add the flour mixture to the liquid mixture. Beat this batter until it is smooth. Pour the batter over the chicken breasts in the casserole dish.

11. Bake the chicken pudding for about 40 minutes, until the batter puffs up and turns golden brown.

12. Have an adult remove the chicken pudding from the oven. Place the pudding on a trivet at the table to serve.

Chicken Houses

Colonists kept chickens in buildings called chicken houses. The houses often had interesting details like the **finial***, or decorative knob, on the roof of the chicken house shown here.*

Hearty main dishes like veal balls were often served at colonial dinners.

Makes 24 veal balls

Ingredients

- 1 pound ground veal
- A few sprigs fresh parsley
- 1 tablespoon minced onion
- ½ teaspoon salt
- ⅛ teaspoon thyme
- ⅛ teaspoon pepper
- ⅛ teaspoon ground cloves
- 1 egg
- 2 tablespoons butter

Equipment

- Large mixing bowl
- Paring knife
- Cutting board
- Measuring spoons
- Wooden spoon
- Plate
- Large skillet
- Serving dish and spoons

Directions

1. Put the ground veal into the mixing bowl.

2. Wash the parsley. Pull off several leaves, and then have an adult help you cut them into small pieces.

3. Add the parsley, minced onion, salt, thyme, pepper, and ground cloves to the veal.

4. Crack the egg into the mixing bowl.

5. Wash your hands. Mix all the ingredients together with your hands, or use the wooden spoon.

6. Shape the meat mixture into 1-inch balls and put them on a plate. Wash your hands after handling the veal balls.

7. With an adult's help, melt the butter in the skillet over medium-low heat. Tilt the skillet to coat the bottom of the pan evenly with butter.

8. Use the wooden spoon to move the veal balls from the plate to the skillet.

9. Cook the veal balls for 30 minutes. Have an adult help you turn the veal balls several times while they cook to brown the meat on all sides.

10. Have an adult help you use 2 spoons to move the cooked veal balls from the skillet to a clean serving dish.

Dish Crosses

In some wealthy households, the most important dish of each course was put in the middle of the table on a dish cross, a stand that raised that dish above the other dishes. The dish cross was made of two crossed bars on short legs. The bars could be shortened or extended to fit almost any size dish.

SWEET POTATOES AND APPLES

Serves 8

Ingredients

- 5 sweet potatoes
- 3 large apples
- Shortening, butter, or cooking spray to grease casserole dish
- 2 tablespoons butter
- ¾ cup maple syrup

Equipment

- Fork
- Cookie sheet
- Pot holders
- Paring knife
- Cutting board
- Paper towels
- Large casserole dish with lid
- Measuring cup and spoon
- Butter knife
- Trivet

To make this tasty dish, Felicity climbed to the roof of her house to pick apples!

Directions

1. Preheat the oven to 350°.

2. Wash the sweet potatoes and pierce each of them several times with a fork. Put them on the cookie sheet and bake them on the center oven rack for about 1 hour, or until a fork pierces them easily.

3. Have an adult remove the potatoes from the oven and set them aside to cool.

4. With an adult's help, cut each apple into 4 sections. Remove the core from each section and cut off the skin. Then cut the apple sections into thin slices.

5. Have an adult help you use the paring knife to pull the skins off the cooked sweet potatoes. Cut the potatoes into ½-inch slices.

6. Use paper towels to grease the casserole dish with shortening or butter, or coat the dish with cooking spray.

7. Use half of the sweet potato slices to cover the bottom of the casserole. Put half the apple slices on top of the potatoes.

8. Use the rest of the sweet potatoes to make the next layer. Then add the rest of the apples.

9. Cut the 2 tablespoons of butter into small pieces and place them on top of the apples. Pour the maple syrup over the top.

10. Cover the casserole and bake the sweet potatoes and apples in the oven for 30 minutes.

11. Have an adult remove the casserole dish from the oven. Place the dish on a trivet at the table to serve.

Root Cellars

Root vegetables, like sweet potatoes, turnips, carrots, and potatoes, were stored in root cellars and covered with sand or dirt. Since root cellars were dug deep into the ground, they stayed cool and kept food from spoiling.

SALLY LUNN BREAD

Makes 1 loaf

Ingredients

- ¾ cup milk
- ¼ cup warm water
- 1 package active dry yeast
- 6 tablespoons butter, softened
- 3 tablespoons sugar
- 2 eggs
- 3 cups flour
- 1¼ teaspoons salt
- Shortening, butter, or cooking spray to grease the pan

Equipment

- Measuring cups and spoons
- Small saucepan
- Small bowl
- Wooden spoon
- Large mixing bowl
- Medium mixing bowl
- Clean kitchen towel
- Paper towels
- Tube pan or round 2-quart casserole dish
- Pot holders
- Butter knife

Rose baked fresh bread for the Merriman family every morning.

Directions

1. Measure the milk into the small saucepan. Have an adult help you heat the milk over medium-low heat. When the milk is warm, but not boiling, turn off the heat.

2. Measure the warm water into the small bowl. Add the yeast and stir. Then have an adult pour the warm milk into the yeast and water. Stir.

3. Measure the butter and sugar into the large mixing bowl. Stir them until they are creamy.

4. Crack 1 egg into the large mixing bowl and beat the mixture. Add the second egg and beat the mixture again.

5. Stir the flour and salt together in the medium mixing bowl.

6. Stir about 1 cup of the flour mixture into the butter and sugar mixture. Then stir in about ⅓ of the yeast mixture.

7. Add more flour and beat the mixture. Then add more yeast and beat the mixture again. Continue adding yeast and flour in this way, beating the batter until it is smooth.

8. Cover the large mixing bowl with a clean towel and let the batter rise in a warm place for 1 hour. When the batter has doubled in size, remove the towel. Stir the batter quickly to take out the air.

9. Use paper towels to grease the tube pan or round casserole dish with shortening or butter, or coat the pan with cooking spray.

10. Pour the batter into the baking pan. Cover it with the towel. Let it rise for about 30 minutes, or until it has doubled again in size. Preheat the oven to 350° while the batter rises.

11. Remove the towel and bake the bread on the center oven rack for 40 to 45 minutes.

12. Have an adult take the bread out of the oven. Use the butter knife to loosen the bread from the sides of the pan. Turn the pan upside down to remove the bread.

Sun-Moon Bread

Some people say Sally Lunn bread came from the French phrase for sun-moon, soleil-lune (so-lay-LOON). Each loaf has a golden top (sun) and white bottom (moon). In English, soleil-lune became "Sally Lunn," which is how the bread is known today.

Green Beans

Serves 6

Ingredients

- 1 pound fresh green beans
- ½ cup cold water
- ½ teaspoon salt
- 1 tablespoon butter
- Salt and pepper
- ¼ cup heavy whipping cream

Equipment

- Colander
- Measuring cups and spoons
- 2-quart saucepan with lid
- Wooden spoon
- Serving bowl and spoon

Felicity picked fresh green beans from the kitchen garden.

Directions

1. Put the beans into the colander and wash them at the sink.

2. Snap off both ends of the beans with your fingers.

3. Put the water and ½ teaspoon salt into the saucepan. With an adult's help, heat the water over medium-high heat until it *boils*, or bubbles rapidly.

4. Put the beans into the water. Cover the saucepan and cook the beans for 5 minutes.

5. Have an adult help you pour the beans and water into the colander. After the water has drained off, put the beans back into the saucepan.

6. Add the butter. Sprinkle on salt and pepper. Add the cream and stir gently to coat the beans well.

7. Spoon the beans into a bowl and serve.

WHIPPED SYLLABUB

"Bub" is an English nickname for a drink with bubbles!

Serves 6

Ingredients

- 2 cups heavy whipping cream
- 2 lemons
- 1 orange
- ½ cup sugar
- ¼ cup sparkling white grape juice

Equipment

- Measuring cups
- Large mixing bowl
- Wire whisk or egg-beater
- Sharp knife
- Cutting board
- Fruit juicer
- Small mixing bowl
- Mixing spoon
- 6 glasses

Directions

1. Measure the whipping cream into the large mixing bowl and beat it with the wire whisk or eggbeater until it is thick. Set the bowl aside.

2. Have an adult help you cut the lemons and orange in half.

3. Set the juicer over the small mixing bowl so that the edges fit tightly.

4. Squeeze the juice out of the lemons and orange by turning them back and forth on the juicer while you push down.

5. Add the sugar and grape juice to the lemon and orange juice. Stir until blended.

6. Pour the juice mixture into the whipped cream. Stir just enough to blend the juices and cream. The syllabub should be thick and frothy. Serve it in individual glasses.

33

FAVORITE FOODS

Beefsteak Pie

•

Baked Pumpkin Pudding

•

Raspberry Flummery

•

Almond Tarts

•

Spiced Nuts

•

Liberty Tea

FAVORITE FOODS

Felicity practiced the tea ceremony at the home of Miss Manderly, her teacher. She loved to watch Miss Manderly gracefully scoop the dry tea leaves into the delicate china teapot. Along with tea, Miss Manderly sometimes served two of Felicity's favorite sweets—tiny almond tarts and queen cakes filled with dark currants.

When the king of England placed a tax on tea, many colonial families, including the Merrimans, protested it. Colonists who did not agree with the king's rule were called *Patriots*. They refused to buy, sell, or drink tea. Instead, they made their own "liberty teas" from flowers, herbs, and fruit leaves. They also drank coffee and chocolate. In Felicity's time, chocolate was a drink, not a candy! A girl like Felicity would shave part of a roll or cake of solid chocolate into boiling water or milk. Then she served the drink from a chocolate pot.

A young girl adding sugar to her tea

When Felicity visited Grandfather's plantation each summer, she was treated to delicious fruit desserts. The woods were thick with wild raspberries and blackberries, strawberries grew near the fields, and watermelons and muskmelons ripened in the melon patch.

In her own garden, Felicity grew vegetables and herbs, just as Grandfather had taught her. She was most pleased with her pumpkins, which were used to make her favorite dessert—baked pumpkin pudding!

BEEFSTEAK PIE

Serves 6

Ingredients

- Two pastry piecrusts for 9-inch pie pan
- 1- to 2-pound beef rump roast
- Salt and pepper
- 1 tablespoon cooking oil
- 2 tablespoons flour
- 4 tablespoons water
- 2 cups beef broth
- 1 teaspoon dried parsley
- ⅛ teaspoon marjoram
- ⅛ teaspoon savory
- ⅛ teaspoon thyme
- 2 tablespoons butter

Equipment

- 9-inch pie pan
- Sharp knife
- Cutting board
- Rolling pin
- Measuring cup and spoons
- Large skillet
- Fork
- Small bowl
- Wooden spoon
- Butter knife
- Pot holders
- Trivet

Colonists ate beefsteak pie warm for dinner and cold for supper or breakfast!

Directions *Have an adult help you with all the steps in this recipe.*

1. Line the bottom of the pie pan with one of the piecrusts.

2. Slice the rump roast into small, thin steaks about ¼ inch thick.

3. Put the steaks on a cutting board or counter and pound them with the rolling pin until they are tender. Sprinkle both sides of the steaks with salt and pepper.

4. Heat the cooking oil in the skillet over medium heat. Put the steaks into the skillet. Use the fork to turn over the steaks several times to brown them on both sides. Use the fork to move the steaks into the pastry-lined pie pan. Set the pan aside.

5. Preheat the oven to 400°. Measure the flour and water into the bowl and stir with the fork to make a smooth paste.

6. Measure the beef broth into the skillet and heat it until it *boils*, or bubbles quickly.

7. To make a gravy, stir the flour paste slowly into the broth with the wooden spoon. When the gravy is thick, turn down the heat. Let the gravy *simmer*, or bubble gently, for 3 minutes.

8. Sprinkle salt and pepper over the gravy and stir. Pour the gravy over the steaks in the pie pan.

9. Sprinkle parsley, marjoram, savory, and thyme over the steaks and gravy.

10. Cut the butter into small pieces. Dot the top of the pie with butter.

11. Cover the pie with the other piecrust. Press the edges of the bottom and top crusts together to seal them. Cut six small slits in the top of the piecrust.

12. Bake the pie for 50 minutes, or until the crust is golden brown. Remove the pie from the oven. Place the pie on a trivet at the table and serve. 🐚

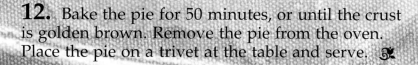

Preserving Meats

Colonists often preserved fresh meat for winter by salting it. First the meat was salted on both sides. Then it was buried under salt in a trough like the one shown here for up to six weeks. After that, colonists either smoked the meat or put it into barrels of salty water, or brine, where the meat soaked until they were ready to cook it.

BAKED PUMPKIN PUDDING

Serves 6

Ingredients

- 4 eggs
- 1-pound can pumpkin
- 1 teaspoon cinnamon
- ½ teaspoon ginger
- ¼ teaspoon allspice
- ½ cup molasses
- 1 cup milk
- Butter, shortening, or cooking spray to grease casserole dish

Equipment

- Large mixing bowl
- Fork
- Wooden spoon
- Measuring cups and spoons
- Paper towels
- 1½-quart casserole dish
- Pot holders
- Knife
- Serving spoon

Felicity used her best pumpkin to make this tasty pudding.

Directions

1. Preheat the oven to 350°.

2. Crack the eggs into the large mixing bowl. Beat them with the fork until they are light yellow. Add the canned pumpkin to the eggs and mix well with the wooden spoon.

3. Measure the cinnamon, ginger, and allspice into the mixing bowl. Add the molasses and milk. Stir well.

4. Use paper towels to grease the casserole dish with butter or shortening, or coat the dish with cooking spray. Pour the pumpkin mixture into the casserole dish.

5. Bake the pudding for 1 hour. Have an adult take the casserole dish out of the oven. If a knife inserted into the center comes out clean, the pudding is done. If not, bake the pudding for a few more minutes, and then try the knife test again. ❧

RASPBERRY FLUMMERY

Flummery was often the featured dessert at the end of an elegant dinner.

Serves 6

Ingredients

- 3 cups raspberries
- ¾ cup cold water
- 1 cup sugar
- ½ teaspoon salt
- 6 tablespoons cornstarch

Equipment

- Colander
- Measuring cups and spoons
- 3-quart saucepan with lid
- Wooden spoon
- Small bowl
- Fork
- 6 small glass dishes

Directions

1. Put the raspberries into the colander and rinse them under cold running water at the sink.

2. Measure the water into the saucepan. Add the berries. Turn the heat to medium high.

3. Cover the saucepan and cook the berries about 10 minutes, or until they are soft. Have an adult help you stir the berries once or twice while they cook.

4. While the berries are cooking, measure the sugar, salt, and cornstarch into the bowl and stir them with the fork.

5. Have an adult help you slowly add the sugar mixture to the cooked berries and stir. Turn the heat to low and cook the mixture for another 10 minutes, or until it becomes thick.

6. With an adult's help, spoon the flummery into glass dishes. Chill the dishes in the refrigerator before serving.

Fancy Flummery

Colonial cooks shaped flummery in jelly molds, and they tinted it, too. Spinach juice created a green tint, syrup of violets made blue, egg yolks made yellow, chocolate made brown, and cream made white. One cook molded flummery into fish shapes. She served the fish in a "pond" of clear jelly!

ALMOND TARTS

Makes 12 tarts

Ingredients

Pastry:
- ¾ cup flour
- 6 tablespoons butter
- 1 egg
- 1 tablespoon cream
- Extra flour for rolling out dough

Filling:
- ½ cup butter
- 1 lemon
- 3 eggs
- 1 cup ground almonds
- 1 tablespoon orange juice
- ½ cup sugar

Equipment

- Measuring cups and spoons
- Medium mixing bowl
- Pastry cutter or fork
- Wooden spoon
- Small saucepan
- Grater
- Large mixing bowl
- Cutting board
- Rolling pin
- Muffin pan
- Butter knife
- Pot holders
- Wire cooling racks

Felicity baked tarts in tiny pans made of tin, brass, or stoneware.

Directions

1. To make the pastry dough, measure the flour and butter into the medium mixing bowl. Use the pastry cutter or fork to blend them until the mixture is crumbly.

2. Crack the egg into the bowl. Add the cream and stir to form a smooth dough.

3. Chill the pastry dough for 15 to 30 minutes in the refrigerator.

4. While the dough is chilling, preheat the oven to 325°.

5. To make the filling, have an adult help you melt the butter in the saucepan over low heat.

✋ **6.** With an adult's help, grate the *rind*, or the outside of the lemon. Measure 1 tablespoon of lemon rind into the large mixing bowl.

7. Crack the eggs into the bowl. Add the melted butter, ground almonds, orange juice, eggs, and sugar. Mix well. Set the bowl aside.

8. Remove the pastry dough from the refrigerator. Divide it into 12 pieces. Shape each piece into a ball.

9. On a floured cutting board, roll out each ball into a thin circle, about ¼ inch thick.

10. Fit each circle into a cup in the muffin pan. Pat the sides to make them fit like tiny piecrusts.

11. Put 2 tablespoons of filling into each muffin cup. Divide any remaining filling evenly among the cups.

12. Bake the almond tarts for 40 minutes, or until a knife inserted in the center of one tart comes out clean.

✋ **13.** Have an adult remove the tarts from the oven. Let them cool in the pan for 10 minutes. With an adult's help, remove the tarts from the muffin pan. Let them cool completely on the wire racks before serving. 🍴

SPICED NUTS

Ingredients

- Shortening, butter, or cooking spray to grease cookie sheets
- 1 cup sugar
- 4 tablespoons cinnamon
- ¼ teaspoon nutmeg
- 2 eggs
- 1 cup pecans
- 1 cup almonds

Equipment

- 2 cookie sheets
- Paper towels
- Measuring cup and spoons
- 2 small bowls
- Spoon
- Fork
- Slotted spoon
- Pot holders
- Nut or candy dish

Sugary, spicy nuts were the perfect ending to any colonial meal.

Directions

1. Preheat the oven to 300°. Use paper towels to grease the cookie sheets with shortening or butter, or coat the sheets with cooking spray.

2. Measure the sugar, cinnamon, and nutmeg into one of the small bowls and mix them with the spoon.

3. Have an adult help you separate the egg whites into the other small bowl. Beat the egg whites with the fork.

4. Stir a few nuts into the egg whites. Then roll the nuts in the sugar and spice mixture.

5. Use a slotted spoon to remove the nuts from the spice mixture. Place the nuts on the cookie sheet. Prepare the rest of the nuts in the same way.

6. Bake the spiced nuts for 20 minutes. With an adult's help, stir the nuts every 5 minutes. Have an adult remove the cookie sheets from the oven. Let the nuts cool before serving them in a dish.

LIBERTY TEA

Felicity made tea from raspberry leaves to protest the high tax on tea that came from England.

Directions

1. Pour the water into a teakettle or saucepan. Heat the water on high heat until it *boils*, or bubbles quickly.

2. Measure the raspberry leaves into the tea ball and place the ball in the teapot. Or measure the raspberry leaves directly into the teapot. Have an adult pour the boiling water into the teapot. Let the tea steep for 5 minutes.

3. Remove the tea ball from the teapot and pour the tea into teacups. Or use the strainer to catch the tea leaves as you pour the tea into teacups. Sweeten the tea with honey.

Serves 6

Ingredients

- 6 cups water
- 3 teaspoons dried raspberry leaves*
- Honey

Equipment

- Teakettle or saucepan
- Measuring cup and spoons
- Tea ball (optional)
- Teapot
- Strainer (if you don't use a tea ball)
- 6 teacups

*Available at health-food stores

Tea Bowls

Families like the Merrimans had teatime each day, between dinner in the early afternoon and supper later in the evening. They drank their tea from cups that had no handles, often called tea bowls.

43

Miss Jennifer Warren
presents her compliments
to Miss Julie Rodgers and
requests the favour of her
attendance at Valentine's
Cake and Party at
...meadow Road
...April 1994

Helena

Clarissa

FELICITY'S COLONIAL TEA

In Virginia, colonists loved to get together for elegant teas, balls, and other celebrations. They dressed in their fanciest clothes and served their favorite sweets on fine china. Then they played games or danced. Some of their parties lasted for days!

Parchment Invitation

Use tan paper that looks like parchment, which was common in Felicity's time. Practice the fancy letters and numbers from the back of the book. Write the invitation in your best handwriting, roll it up, and tie it with a ribbon.

Stenciled Name Cards

Fold a 4-by-4-inch piece of paper in half. Tape a small stencil to one corner, leaving room for the name. Use a small sponge to lightly paint the open areas of the stencil. Let the paint dry, and remove the stencil. Write your guest's name on the card.

Fruit Pyramid Centerpiece

Place a Styrofoam cone (available at craft stores) on a dinner plate. Have an adult cut off the point of the cone. Attach fruit to the cone with toothpicks or wooden skewers. Use evergreen boughs, herb sprigs, or other greens to fill the spaces between the fruit.

QUEEN CAKES

Makes 12 cakes

Ingredients

- Shortening, butter, or cooking spray to grease pan
- Flour to coat greased pan
- ½ cup butter, softened
- ½ cup sugar
- 2 eggs
- 2 tablespoons rose water*
- ¼ teaspoon mace
- ¼ teaspoon salt
- 1 cup flour
- 1 tablespoon flour
- ¼ cup currants

Equipment

- Paper towels
- Muffin pans
- Measuring cups and spoons
- Medium mixing bowl
- Wooden spoon
- Small bowl
- Pot holders

*Rosewater is available at health-food stores and some supermarkets. If you can't find it, substitute 1 teaspoon of vanilla extract and 2 teaspoons of water.

Dainty queen cakes make delightful party treats. Serve them with Liberty Tea (page 43).

Directions

1. Preheat the oven to 325°. Use paper towels to grease the muffin pans with shortening or butter, or coat the pan with cooking spray. Then coat each muffin cup with flour.

2. Put the softened butter into the mixing bowl. Add the sugar and stir the mixture until it is creamy.

3. Crack the eggs into the mixing bowl 1 at a time. Beat the mixture after adding each egg.

46

4. Add the rose water, mace, and salt. Beat well.

5. Add 1 cup of flour to the mixture, ¼ cup at a time. Each time you add flour, beat the mixture until you have a smooth batter.

6. Put 1 tablespoon of flour into the small bowl. Add the currants and stir to coat them with flour. Then stir the currants into the batter.

7. Fill each muffin cup ½ full.

8. Bake the queen cakes for 40 minutes, or until they are golden brown.

9. Have an adult remove the queen cakes from the oven. Use a butter knife to loosen the cakes from the muffin cups and move them to a serving plate.

Sugar Cones

In 1774, white sugar was pressed into a cone shape and packaged in blue paper. Colonial cooks pinched chunks of sugar from the cone with sugar nips, which look like tongs. No one knows why the wrapper was always blue, but colonists often soaked the color out of the paper and used it to dye fabric.

Rose Water

Rose water was a popular flavoring in Felicity's day. It was made by boiling rose petals in water.

Miss Sarah Mayer
presents her compliments
to Miss Michelle Andrews and
requests the favor of her
attendance at Felicity's
New Year's Ball at
356 Hill Avenue
on Saturday,
January 3rd
at 6:00 in
the evening.

Twelfth Night

Colonists in Virginia celebrated Christmastide from mid-December until January 6, twelve days after Christmas. It was common to have a final party on this day, which was called *Twelfth Night*. Festivities often included a fancy meal and a ball. Try some of these party ideas at your next holiday or New Year's Eve party. Or host a fancy, festive ball for no reason at all!

Fan Invitation

Trace the fan pattern from the back of the book for each invitation. Tape the pattern to a piece of light-colored paper. Cut it out. Write the invitation on one side of the fan. Copy the fancy letters and numbers from the back of the book if you like. Then decorate both sides of the fan. Fold it in half lengthwise and tie a ribbon around the bottom. Deliver the invitation by hand, just as Felicity would have done.

✋ Twelfth Night Cake

Twelfth Night was celebrated with a special cake. It usually had smooth white icing and was decorated with colorful candied flowers and fruits. Have an adult help you make your favorite cake recipe, or prepare a boxed cake mix. Just before you put the batter into the oven, drop in a dried bean. Bake the cake according to the directions. Once it has cooled, add icing and candy decorations. The person who finds the bean is the queen of the feast!

New Year's Cookies

In colonial times, these cookies were made to celebrate the New Year. Have an adult help you make your favorite sugar cookie recipe, or buy a package of refrigerated cookie dough. Roll out the dough. Use the cookie cutter that came with *Felicity's Cooking Studio* to cut out tulip shapes, or use any cookie cutter shape you like. In a small bowl, mix 2 teaspoons of nutmeg and 2 tablespoons of sugar. Sprinkle the sugar mixture on the cut-out cookies. Have an adult help you bake them according to the directions.

Felicity's Flowers

Felicity took great pride in her garden. She loved tending to the sweet-smelling flowers that grew in elegant, orderly rows along with the herbs and vegetables.

Minuet

Grace is the key for this "queen of dances"!

1. Stand next to your partner and hold hands. Both of you walk forward—left, right, left. Point your right toes. Walk forward again, starting with your right feet.

2. Face your partner and hold hands. Step on your left feet and swing your right feet forward. Step on your right feet and swing your left feet forward.

3. One partner lets go with her right hand, raises her left arm, and twirls her partner under her arm.

4. Repeat steps 1 to 3. Once you have the steps down, repeat them to music. Look for recordings of classical music by Bach or Mozart at your library.

PLANTATION PICNIC

Sweet-Smelling Invitation

Write out each invitation on a small card. Put it in an envelope and sprinkle dried potpourri inside. Or punch a hole in the card, thread a ribbon through it, and tie the ribbon around a flower.

Cranberry-Apple Punch

Mix together 2 quarts of cranberry juice, 2 cups of apple juice, and 2 cups of lemonade. Pour the punch into a pretty pitcher, add ice, and it's ready to serve.

Chicken Salad

Have an adult help you chop 2 celery ribs and 4 hard-boiled eggs. Combine the celery, eggs, and 4 cups chopped cooked or canned chicken in a mixing bowl. In a separate small bowl, mix ⅓ cup mayonnaise, 1 teaspoon Dijon mustard, 1 teaspoon dried tarragon, and salt and pepper to taste. Mix well. Add the dressing to the chicken mixture. Refrigerate it until it's time to eat. Serve it on sandwiches or scooped on beds of lettuce.

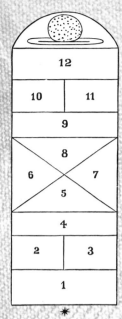

Scotch-Hoppers

Felicity called hopscotch "scotch-hoppers." Use chalk to draw this colonial hopscotch pattern on the sidewalk or driveway. Take turns tossing a stone and hopping to the top!

Bowls

Divide your guests into 2 teams. Each team gets 4 *bowls*, or balls, such as croquet balls. Throw a *jack*, or smaller target ball, onto the lawn. The teams stand at a starting line and take turns rolling their bowls as close to the jack as they can. The team with the bowl closest to the jack wins.

Battledore and Shuttlecock

In colonial days, badminton was called "battledore and shuttlecock." If colonial children didn't have a battledore, or racket, they used their school hornbooks as rackets! Felicity might have said this rhyme as she played. Say a line with each swing, and keep repeating it until the shuttlecock falls.

A hornbook

One, two, three, four,
Mary at the cottage door,
Eating cherries off a plate,
Five, six, seven, eight.

Questions or comments? Call 1-800-845-0005,
visit our Web site at **americangirl.com**, or write to Customer Service,
American Girl, 8400 Fairway Place, Middleton, WI 53562-0497.

Printed in China
07 08 09 10 11 12 13 LEO 12 11 10 9 8 7 6 5 4 3 2

PICTURE CREDITS
The following individuals and organizations have generously given permission to reprint illustrations in this book:
p. 4—from *Home Life in Colonial Days* by Alice Morse Earle, © 1954, The Macmillan Company; p. 5—Wisconsin Historical Society;
p. 7—Courtesy, Winterthur Museum; pp. 8–13—Colonial Williamsburg Foundation; p. 15—Library of Congress; p. 17—Courtesy,
Mount Vernon Ladies' Association; p. 19—Colonial Williamsburg Foundation (smokehouse); p. 23—Courtesy, Winterthur Museum;
p. 25—from *Back of the Big House: The Architecture of Plantation Slavery* by John Michael Vlach, copyright © 1993 by the University of
North Carolina Press; p. 27—Colonial Williamsburg Foundation; p. 35—National Gallery of Art; p. 37—from *Back of the Big House:
The Architecture of Plantation Slavery* by John Michael Vlach, copyright © 1993 by the University of North Carolina Press; p. 39—Talbot
County Historical Society; p. 43—Courtesy of Trustees, Victoria & Albert Museum; p. 47—Colonial Williamsburg (sugar cone);
p. 51—*Girl with Racket and Shuttlecock*, © 1740 (oil on canvas), Chardin, Jean-Baptiste Simeon (1699–1779), Galleria degli Uffizi,
Florence, Italy, The Bridgeman Art Library.

Edited by Jodi Goldberg, Jeanne Thieme, and Teri Witkowski
Written by Polly Athan, Rebecca Sample Bernstein, Terri Braun, Jodi Goldberg, and Jeanne Thieme
Designed and art directed by Justin King
Produced by Jeannette Bailey, Mary Cudnohfsky, Julie Kimmell, Judith Lary, and Gail Longworth
Cover illustration by Dan Andreasen
Interior illustrations by Susan Mahal
Photography by Mark Salisbury
Historical and picture research by Polly Athan, Rebecca Sample Bernstein, Terri Braun,
Jodi Goldberg, Robyn Hansen, Doreen Smith, and Sally Wood
Recipe testing coordinated by Jean doPico
Food styling by Janice Bell
Prop research by Leslie Cakora

Fan Invitation

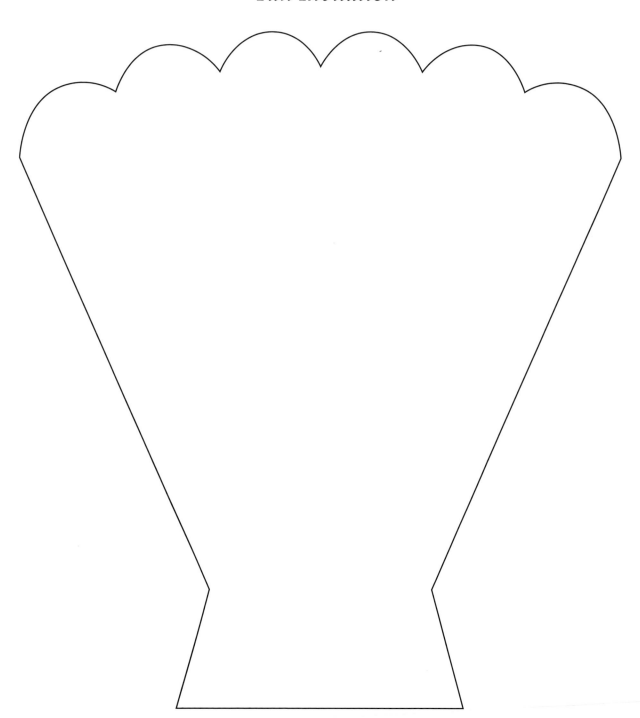

Alphabet

A B C D E F G
H I J K L M
N O P Q R S T
U V W X Y Z

a b c d e f g h i j k l m
n o p q r s t u v w x y z
1 2 3 4 5 6 7 8 9 0